It's
Great
to Be
Catholic!

By Susan Heyboer O'Keefe

Illustrations by Patrick Kelley

Paulist Press
New York/Mahwah, N.J.

Cover and book design by Saija Autrand, Faces Type & Design

Library of Congress Cataloging-in-Publication Data

O'Keefe, Susan Heyboer.
    It's great to be Catholic! / by Susan Heyboer O'Keefe ; illustrated by Patrick Kelley.
      p.   cm.
    ISBN 0-8091-6680-1
    1. Christian children—Religious life—Juvenile literature.   2. Catholic Church—Doctrines—Juvenile literature.   3. Catholic Church—Membership—Juvenile literature. [1. Catholic Church.]
  I. Kelley, Patrick, 1963- ill. II. Title.

BX2371 .O54 2000
282—dc21

                                        00-049157

Published by Paulist Press
997 Macarthur Boulevard
Mahwah, New Jersey 07430

www.paulistpress.com

Printed and bound in Mexico

For the many people
at St. John the Evangelist Church
who have shown me that
"It's great to be Catholic!"

S.H.O'K.

To the BVM,
Totus Tuus, Too.

P.K.

What makes being Catholic great?
Lots of little things—

Incense, bells, and candles,
Feathery angel wings,

Stained glass in the morning,
A rosary to hold tight,

A priest up at the altar
In purple, green, or white.

What makes being Catholic great?
Lots of little things—

Playing with the Christmas crib,
The camels, and the kings,

Staying up for Midnight Mass
Long past the time for bed,

Skipping meat on Fridays
To have grilled cheese instead. . . .

Dressing up like brides and grooms
On First Communion Day,

Making chains of daisies
For Mary's crown in May,

Helping fill up Noah's ark
With pets that never bite,

Then drawing pictures of the saints
With halos shining bright.

What makes being Catholic great?
Lots of *big* things, too—

Knowing Baby Jesus
Grew up like me and you,

Hearing how he saved us
By dying on the tree,

And now is always with us
As real as you or me. . . .

Reading in the Bible
Good News for every day,
Finding full forgiveness
Those times we disobey,

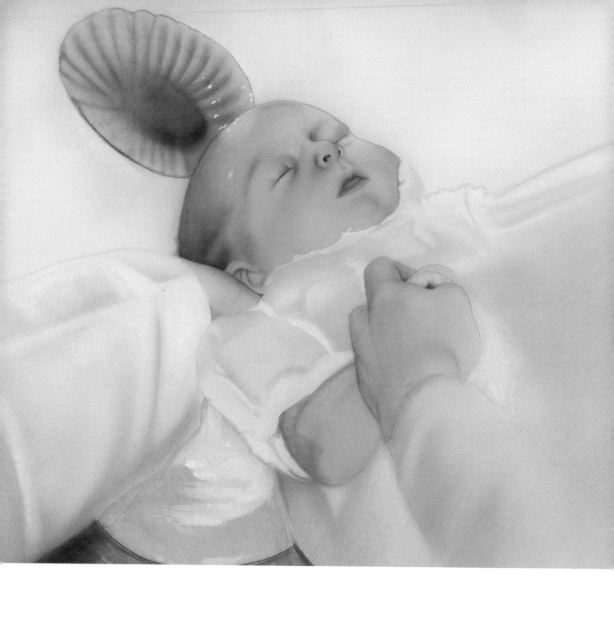

Having seven sacraments
To mark the road ahead—

Like when a baby's baptized
Or a man and woman wed,

Seeing just one family
In every different face,

Winning life in heaven
To rest in God's embrace.

What makes being Catholic great?
Knowing it's so true

That God is good, and so are we,
And every day's brand new,

That every life's important,
And God loves each the same,

No matter our religion,
Our color, or our name.

I love being Catholic
Every single day!
It's how I show my love for God
In an extra-special way.